FLynn.S

my first
Science
BOOK

ARCTURUS

ARCTURUS

This edition published in 2019 by Arcturus Publishing Limited
26/27 Bickels Yard, 151–153 Bermondsey Street,
London SE1 3HA

Illustrator: Samantha Meredith
Author: Jacqueline McCann
Consultant: Helen Lewis
Designer: Ms Mousepenny

ISBN: 978-1-78950-313-5
CH007015UK
Supplier 33, Date 0719, Print run 9125

Printed in China

Marvellous Materials

Look at the things around you. They are all made of something, and that something is called a material. There are lots of different kinds of materials.

 This is a chair. →  It is made of wood. → Wood comes from trees.

 This is a can. It is made from a mixture of metals. → Metals come from rocks, called ore. →  Rocks are dug up from the ground.

 These are a pair glasses. → Glass is made of sand. → Sand comes from the sea, beaches, dunes and rocks.

 This is a pair of denim jeans. →  Denim is made of cotton. → Cotton comes from a plant.

 This is a jug. → The jug is made from clay. →  Clay is a type of rocky soil dug from the earth.

Where Did It Come From?

Can you guess what material each object is made from?

a

b

c

d

e

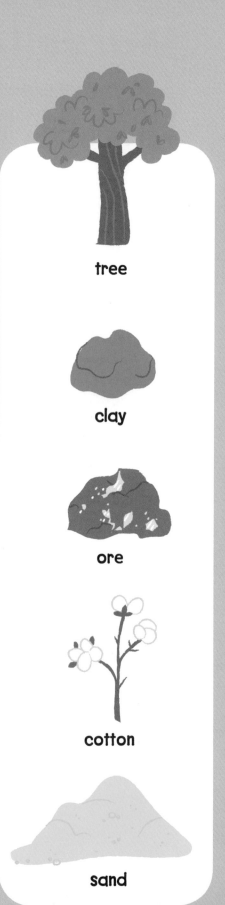

tree

clay

ore

cotton

sand

Build Me!

What would you use to make the things that are labelled on this house? Choose the best material from the objects in the panel below.

drainpipe

roof

wall

veranda

door

slate   bricks   straw   wood   stone   sticks   plastic

Look Around

Take a look at your kitchen. Everything you see is made from one or more materials. Some materials are better than others – it depends what job you want them to do.

Glass is clear. You can see through it and it is smooth.

Rubber gloves are light, bendy and waterproof.

Metal is strong. It won't break.

A stone counter is hard and won't scratch easily.

A wool jumper is soft and warm.

A plastic bowl is waterproof and strong. It won't leak and it won't break easily.

This wooden table is stiff, strong and hard.

Think Like a Designer

Imagine you have a job designing everyday things. What do you think the following objects should be made from? Choose from the following: clay, cotton, metal, plastic, rubber, wood.

1

2

3

4

5

6

7

8

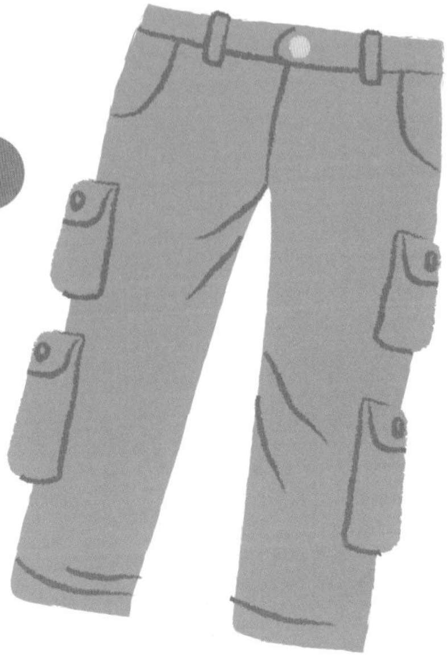

9

Solids, Liquids and Gases

All materials can be described as one of these three things: a solid, gas or liquid.

A solid keeps its shape and you can hold it – if it's small enough!

phone

tree trunk

brick

die

A gas can be invisible, which means you can't see it. It doesn't have a fixed shape.

helium gas inside the balloon

water vapour

A liquid flows and can be poured easily. It is not easy to hold. It changes shape to fill the container it is in.

water

juice

custard

Help the Teacher

The teacher is trying to explain the differences between liquids, solids and gases. Can you draw a line from each object to the correct heading?

Liquid **Solid** **Gas**

exhaust fumes

milk

runny honey

wooden spoon

hair clip

gas

tea

breaking wind!

Fizzy Water

book

bubbles in fizzy water

air

9

Heating Up, Cooling Down

Solids, liquids and gases don't always stay the way they are. If you heat ice (a solid) it turns into water (a liquid). When the water (liquid) cools down and freezes, it turns back into ice (solid).

Heat turns liquid water into water vapour, which is a gas. Water vapour is invisible.

When water vapour touches the air, it cools down. It turns into tiny droplets of liquid water. This is steam.

A gas can become a solid too, when cold water vapour freezes on a window in winter.

If you heat some solids, they turn into liquids. Butter goes runny when you heat it.

Freezing and Melting

These penguins are experimenting with water and ice. Can you match the descriptions to each picture?

1

When ice melts, it turns to water.

2

When water freezes, it turns to ice.

Rocking Rocks

The Earth's surface is made of rock that lies just below the ground. People have been digging up rocks for thousands of years! There are many different kinds and some are harder than others.

Sandstone is good for building. It is soft enough to carve.

Marble is a beautiful, hard rock. It is good for sculpture and table tops.

Chalk is a soft, white rock. It's perfect for writing and drawing on a blackboard!

Granite is a very hard rock made of differently shaded grains that have sharp edges.

The Right Rock

Look at the finished objects and see if you can figure out which kind of rock they are made from.

 **Chalk** is soft enough for writing.

 **Sandstone** is strong enough for building.

 **Marble** looks beautiful to artists.

 **Granite** is tough enough for walking on.

1

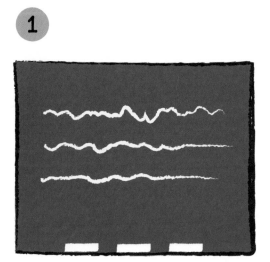

2

3

4

Simply Soil

Resting on top of all the rock on Earth is a layer of soil. Soil is made of bits of rock and dead plants, together with water, air and tiny living creatures, such as animals and fungi. They all provide important things which help plants to grow.

The top layer is called the topsoil. It is usually dark brown. There are lots of bits of fungi, animals and dead plants here.

The next layer is the subsoil. The subsoil doesn't have many dead plants. There is lots of clay and it is usually light brown.

The layer called the parent rock has lots of stones. Very few dead plants are found here.

A layer called bedrock lies at the bottom. It is solid rock.

14

Clear as Mud!

The Earth is covered in many different kinds of soil, which help plants grow. Trace the lines to match the descriptions to the pictures.

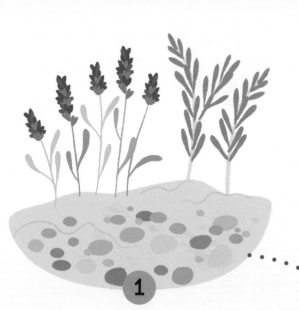

1

Peaty soil is dark brown and crumbly. It doesn't contain many stony bits. It's made from rotting plants from long ago.

2

Chalky soil is light brown. Water passes through it quickly.

3

Sandy soil is pale. It has chunky bits in it and lots of air gaps. Water passes through it easily. It feels quite dry.

Clay soil is sticky and has small bits in it. There are very few air gaps. Water does not pass through it easily.

4

Seasons

Throughout the year, there are times when the weather gets hotter, colder or wetter. These are the seasons and they happen because the Earth tilts slightly as it travels around the Sun.

Winter in the Northern Hemisphere

When the northern part of Earth tilts away from the Sun, it receives less heat and light and so it is colder. Then it is wintertime in the North and summer in the South.

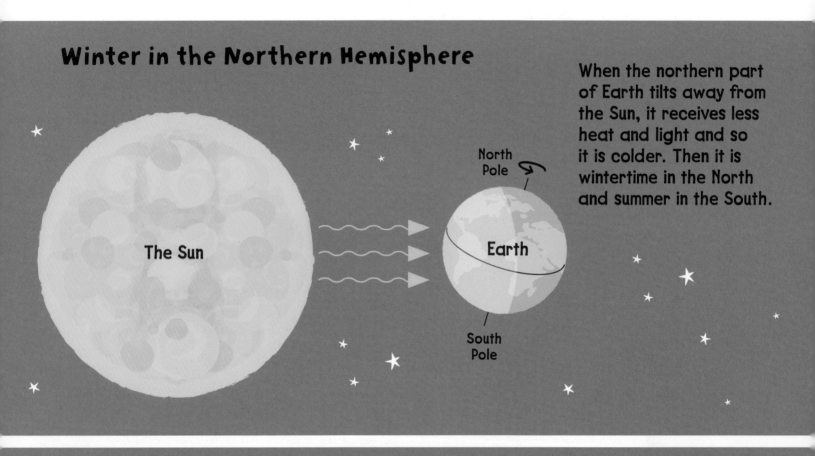

The Sun

North Pole

Earth

South Pole

Summer in the Northern Hemisphere

When the northern part of Earth tilts towards the Sun, it receives more heat and light and so it is warmer. Then it is summertime in the North.

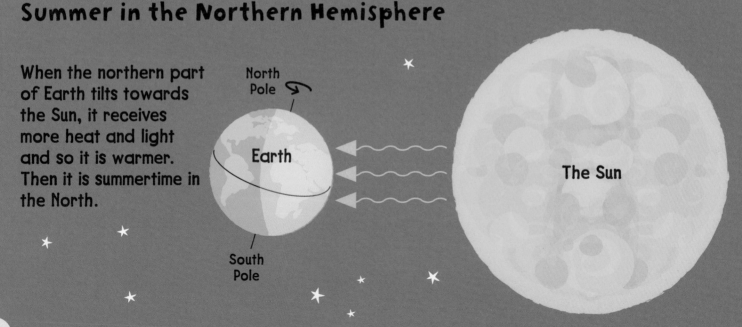

North Pole

Earth

South Pole

The Sun

Look Up!

When you get out of bed in the morning and look up at the sky, what you see is the weather. Look at these pictures and match them to the descriptions at the bottom of the page.

a

b

c

d

e

f

Raining

Stormy

Cold and Snowing

Cold but not Snowing

Cold and windy

Warm and sunny

Whatever the Weather

Weather may be hot, cold, windy, icy or thundery. Weather changes with the seasons, and from country to country.

When the wind blows, the air may feel cold or warm. Sometimes it's a sign that rain, or a storm, is on the way.

On a sunny day in summer, the air feels hot.

In wintertime, the weather can be cold and icy.

When it's very cloudy, some clouds may reach the ground – that's fog!

When clouds appear, they often bring rain and wet weather.

When the weather is ice cold, rain turns to hail.

What to Wear

We wear certain clothes depending on the weather. Can you tell which clothes go with rain, sun or snow?

1

2

rain

3

4

5

sun

7

6

snow

9

8

Cloudy Day

Clouds are made of tiny drops of water. They are constantly changing and moving across the sky.

Thin, wispy clouds high in the sky are made of ice.

On a fine, sunny day, you may see clouds that look like fluffy balls of cotton wool.

Low, dark clouds may be a sign that it's going to rain. They may hide more clouds above.

Fog is cloud that forms near the ground. If you walk through fog, you're walking through a cloud!

Weather Words

Some of these words describe the weather, and others don't. Can you circle all of the weather words?

quiet

cloudy

icy

drizzle

rainy

windy

hot

stripy

leafy

misty

noisy

breezy

blue

foggy

cold

snowy

freezing

smelly

Thunder and Lightning

When rain clouds darken overhead, there is a good chance that a thunderstorm is on the way. Thunder is the loud crashing noise you hear in the sky after lightning strikes!

Lightning is a flash of electricity that happens during thunderstorms. Light flashes between the clouds or travels down towards the ground.

Thunder is the sound made by a bolt of lightning.

Fine to Fly?

Imagine that you're a pilot. Would it be safe for you to fly today? Look out of the window, and then follow the arrows below.

Up, up and away!

Watch out for heavy rain.

A dusting of light cloud just ahead.

Uh oh, thunder and lightning forecast!

Clear blue skies this way.

Fog and mist incoming. Watch out!

Oh no, dark clouds ahead!

Fluffy clouds up above.

Not safe to fly!

Hold on to your hat, it's windy up there!

Very calm, no wind, the coast is clear!

WHAT'S THE WEATHER LIKE TODAY?

START HERE!

ANSWERS

PAGE 4: Where Did It Come From?

(a) **Bricks**: clay

(b) **Wooden spoon**: tree

(c) **Pot**: ore (metal) – and the wooden handle came from a tree

(d) **Drinking glass**: sand

(e) **T-shirt**: cotton

PAGE 5: Build Me!

Roof: slate

Wall: bricks

Door, Veranda: wood

Drainpipe: plastic

PAGE 7: Think Like a Designer

Most of the objects can be made from several different materials! Here is a suggestion.

1. Wood (paper)
2. Clay
3. Wood
4. Cotton
5. Wood
6. Metal and plastic
7. Cotton (and rubber)
8. Cotton
9. Metal

PAGE 9: Help the Teacher

Liquid: honey, milk, tea.

Solid: wooden spoon, hair clip, book

Gas: exhaust fumes, cooking gas, bubbles in fizzy water, breaking wind, air.

PAGE 11: Freezing and Melting

(1) When water freezes, it turns to ice.

(2) When ice melts, it turns to water.

PAGE 13: The Right Rock

Writing on a blackboard: chalk

Grand staircase: granite

Palace: sandstone

Sculpture: marble

PAGE 15: Clear as Mud!

Picture 1: Sandy soil

Picture 2: Clay soil

Picture 3: Chalky soil

Picture 4: Peaty soil

PAGE 17 Look Up!

a: Cold and snowing.

b: Cold but not snowing.

c: Cold and windy.

d: Raining.

e: Stormy – it's raining.

f: Warm and sunny.

PAGE 19: What to Wear

Rain: 2, 4, 5

Sun: 1, 7, 8

Snow: 3, 6, 9

PAGE 21: Weather Words

Weather words: hot, cold, rainy, windy, icy, snowy, drizzle, cloudy, breezy, misty, foggy, freezing

Non-weather words: quiet, noisy, leafy, blue, smelly, stripy

PAGE 23: Fine to Fly?

Your answer will depend on the weather outside your window.

The statements along the right-hand side to the top will get you safely into the sky:

Very calm, no wind, the coast is clear! - Fluffy clouds up above. - Clear blue skies this way. - A dusting of light cloud just ahead. - Up, up and away!